21st CENTURY CITIZEN

Terrorism

Nathaniel Harris

FRANKLIN
WATTS

Titles in this series:
AIDS
Animal Rights
Genetic Engineering
Immigrants and Refugees
Terrorism
World Hunger

© 2004 Arcturus Publishing Ltd

Produced for Franklin Watts by
Arcturus Publishing Ltd, 26/27 Bickels Yard,
151-153 Bermondsey Street, London SE1 3HA.

Series concept: Alex Woolf
Editor: Kelly Davis
Designer: Stonecastle Graphics/Kudos
    Editorial and Design Services
Consultant: James T. Kirkhope
Picture researcher: Shelley Noronha,
    Glass Onion Pictures

Published in the UK by Franklin Watts.

British Library Cataloguing Publication Data
A CIP catalogue record for this book is
available from the British Library.

ISBN 0 7496 5465 1

Printed and bound in Italy

Franklin Watts – the Watts Publishing Group,
96 Leonard Street, London EC2A 4XD.

Picture acknowledgements
Popperfoto 4 (Sean Adair), 8 (Ho, Reuters, 9
(Anatolian), 10 (Jeff Mitchell, Reuters), 19 and
title page, 22-23, 32, 36 (Hector Mata), 37
(Reuters); Rex Features 6 (Ron Sachs), 16 (Sipa
Press), 17, 24 (Sipa Press), 45 (Sipa Press),
Topham 5 (Allan Tannenbaum/The Image
Works), 7 and cover (above), 12, 15, 18, 21 and
cover (below), 27, 29, 31, 35 (Rommel Pecson).

Cover pictures:
Above: Investigators remove debris from the
Sari Club in Kuta, Bali, after the devastating car
bomb attack in October 2002.
Below: Masked Palestinian gunmen flourish
their weaponry on a march in the West Bank
city of Nablus in 2000.

Note to parents and teachers
Some recommended websites are listed under
'Useful Addresses' at the back of this book.
Every effort has been made by the Publishers to
ensure that these websites are suitable for
children; that they are of the highest
educational value; and that they contain no
inappropriate or offensive material. However,
because of the nature of the Internet, it is
impossible to guarantee that the contents of
these sites will not be altered. We strongly
advise that Internet access is supervised by a
responsible adult.

Contents

1: A Global Menace

The first plane crashed into the north tower of the World Trade Center at 8.45 a.m. Most people who saw it or heard about it believed that a terrible accident had happened. But 18 minutes later, a second plane smashed into the south tower. People began to realize that this was a deliberate attack.

The World Trade Center stood on Manhattan Island, at the heart of the USA's largest city, New York. Its twin towers were the tallest structures in New York, 110 storeys high. They dominated the city's famous skyline, seen by every visitor who arrived by land, sea and air. The Center was also an economic powerhouse, which was filled with business companies and thousands of employees from all over the world. It was a symbol of America's immense economic strength, and that was why it was targeted. The USA was not at war with any other country, so there was not much doubt about it – this was a terrorist attack, a murderous, un-lawful assault, carried out with no regard for the loss of innocent lives.

Later, it became fairly clear what had happened. The planes were US passenger airliners making flights across the American continent from the east coast to Los Angeles or San Francisco on the west coast. But in mid-air, American Airlines Flight 11 and United Airlines Flight 175 had been hijacked – taken over by men armed with knives. These men had

The south tower (left) of the World Trade Center bursts into flames after being struck by hijacked United Airlines Flight 175. The north tower is already burning, following an earlier attack by a hijacked airliner.

changed the planes' flight paths and deliberately crashed them into the World Trade Center. This was a suicide attack, since the terrorists who controlled the planes were certain to die as they hit their targets.

The results were horrific. Loaded with fuel, the airliners exploded on impact like bombs. People fled from the buildings, but many were trapped. Policemen and firemen rushed in to help. Many of them were among the dead when, between 10.05 and 10.28, the towers collapsed, sending up vast clouds of dust and smoke.

'9/11'
Two other planes were hijacked the same morning. One, American Airlines Flight 77, crashed into the Pentagon, the headquarters of the US Defense Department, close to the national capital, Washington, DC. Part of the Pentagon building was destroyed and 188 passengers, crew and Pentagon workers were killed.

Shocked survivors flee the collapsed towers of the World Trade Center after the terrorist attack on 11 September 2001.

PERSPECTIVES

'If they're going to crash this plane into the ground, we're going to have to do something... It's up to us. I think we can do it... Don't worry. [Pause] We're going to do something.'

Tom Burnett, one of the passengers on Flight 93 who fought the hijackers, speaking to his wife on a mobile phone, 11 September 2001

The fourth hijacking had a different ending. When the terrorists seized control of United Airlines Flight 93, some of the passengers called their families or friends on mobile phones. When they were told about the attack on the twin towers, they made up their minds not to accept their fate, but to take on the hijackers. The passengers knew they were almost certain to die anyway during the terrorists' suicide mission, but it still took great courage for unarmed people to attack their captors. We do not know exactly what happened next, because the airliner crashed into open land in Pennsylvania and everybody on board was killed. But it is clear that the action taken by the passengers had prevented the hijackers from reaching their suspected destination in Washington, DC. There they would almost certainly have used the plane as a flying bomb against some famous site, claiming many more lives.

Following the events of 9/11, the 'war on terrorism' begins. President George W. Bush, accompanied by US Attorney General John Ashcroft, announces the release of the world's 'Most Wanted Terrorist' list, on 10 October 2001.

In total, the four hijackings led to 2,749 deaths. The date was 11 September 2001 which, shortened to '9/11', has become the name commonly used everywhere for this day of horror.

The 9/11 attack was so devastating that it changed history, leading US President George W. Bush to proclaim a 'war on terrorism'. But 9/11 was not unique. Terrorism had become a serious problem by the 1960s, mainly in the Middle East and Europe. Then, in the 1990s,

the situation seemed to become much worse. Actually, compared with the 1960s, fewer terrorist acts occurred in the 1990s and the early 2000s, but many more people were killed as the attacks became more spectacular, deadly and global. Here are just a few examples.

Investigators remove debris from the Sari Club in Kuta, Bali, after the devastating car bomb attack in October 2002.

In October 2001, soon after 9/11, gunmen attacked the Jammu and Kashmir parliament house in northern India and 38 lives were lost in the violence that followed. On 12 October 2002, terrorists planted bombs at Kuta, a resort on the Indonesian island of Bali. The explosions killed over 202 people, many of them Australian tourists. Less than a fortnight later, terrorists took over a theatre in Moscow, Russia, and held the audience as hostages. The terrorists were killed, but about 119 hostages died (see pages 8, 41 and 43). On 19 August 2003, an attack by a suicide bomber left 23 dead on a bus in Jerusalem, Israel. These events, and many others like them, suggested that terrorism had become a worldwide problem.

What is terrorism?

Terrorism involves the use of violence to spread fear and misery in a society in pursuit of some political aim. (Terrorist acts are not crimes in the ordinary sense – committed for financial gain or a

CASE STUDY

On 23 October 2002, the audience at the Dubrovka Theatre, Moscow, became hostages. The theatre was taken over by terrorists from Chechnya in southern Russia. As well as 21 heavily armed men, there were 19 Chechen women terrorists with explosives strapped to their bodies. The terrorists declared that they would blow up the theatre unless the Russian army was withdrawn from Chechnya. For 57 hours, the hostages lived with terror, confined to their seats. When they wanted to go to the lavatory, they had to use the orchestra pit at the front of the stage. Two people who stumbled into the theatre from outside were shot as spies. 'It froze our hearts,' one woman recalled. As tension mounted, a young boy panicked and ran. The terrorists fired and missed, hitting a man and a woman. Strangely, the terrorists released them, to prove that the wounding had been an accident! The wounded woman survived, unlike her husband and daughter, who remained inside. Fear spread as the terrorist leader became angry. But then the Russian government offered talks. Everybody relaxed – not knowing that a dramatic but disastrously mismanaged rescue was about to begin (see pages 41 and 43).

A still from Russian television network NTV coverage, showing Movsar Barayev (right), leader of the Chechen rebels who took the audience hostage at the Dubrovka Theatre, Moscow, Russia, in October 2002.

personal motive like revenge.) Typical terrorist acts include planting bombs, shooting or kidnapping people, and taking hostages. Perhaps the most important single characteristic of terrorism is that most of its victims are civilians – usually people who have no special political importance and can hardly be seen as the terrorists' enemies.

This targeting of innocent people is what makes terrorists different from rebels (people who fight against their government) or soldiers. Terrorists are not fighting the 'enemy' government, or people, directly. Their tactics are intended to disrupt the normal workings of society. They hope to make life so intolerable that the government will agree to their demands,

or will be replaced, perhaps under pressure from their own frightened citizens, who want the terror to end.

This description of terrorism covers most cases, but not all of them. Rebels or soldiers are fighters, not terrorists. But they may use terrorist methods on occasion, murdering non-combatants or taking hostages who will be killed if the local population refuses to co-operate. For example, groups among the Kurdish people, living in neighbouring regions of Turkey, Iraq and Iran, have adopted various tactics, sometimes including terrorism, in their struggle to achieve a state of their own.

Members of the PKK (Kurdish Workers' Party), captured by Turkish forces in 1995. The PKK used guerrilla (hit and run) warfare and terrorist tactics against Turks and foreign tourists in Turkey until 1999 as part of its struggle for Kurdish independence, brutally suppressed by Turkish security forces.

PERSPECTIVES

'The label "terrorist" often involves a value judgement, in particular whether or not the speaker or writer supports the ultimate goals pursued by the terrorists, such as independence from a colonial power.'

Dr Frank Emmert, Visiting Professor at the Cardozo School of Law, USA, addressing the conference 'Negotiating with Terrorists' at Cardozo in 2003

Government forces may also use terrorist-style tactics against their own people or a foreign population. The word 'terrorism' was actually first used to describe the policy of a government during the French Revolution, which in 1793-4 executed tens of thousands of citizens suspected of working against it. There have been many more recent examples. A group of military men ruled Argentina between 1976 and 1982. During that time, government security forces arrested many thousands of individuals who were never seen again. People in Argentina supposed, correctly, that 'the disappeared' had been executed, but the uncertainty added to the suffering of the victims' families. Such operations are often described as state terrorism. This book is not about state terrorism, but it is important to realize that, in some places, violence by states and their armies has contributed to the existence of equally extreme terrorist responses.

It is not always clear who is, and who is not, a terrorist. Some governments claim that anyone who opposes them is a terrorist. In South Africa, for example, only white people – about a fifth of the population – had any political rights until 1990. Opposition organizations like the African National Congress (ANC) were defined as terrorists and outlawed before they decided to adopt even a limited form of armed struggle, involving sabotage (deliberate destruction of buildings, etc) without violence against people. On the other hand, most terrorists would call themselves freedom fighters, ignoring the fact that there are different ways to struggle for freedom. 'Terrorism' describes the way terrorists try to achieve their aims; whether the aims themselves are worthy is a separate issue.

April 1995: the north side of the federal building in the centre of Oklahoma City; 168 people were killed in the bombing.

PERSPECTIVES

'Those who practise terrorism lose any right to have their cause understood ... We're right, they're wrong. It's as simple as that.'

Rudolph Giuliani, Mayor of New York City, addressing the United Nations Assembly's Special Session on Terrorism on 1 October 2001

A complex subject

Terrorists may be outsiders, or they may be members of the society they attack. The 9/11 atrocity was the work of Al Qaida, an international organization led by Osama bin Laden, originally a Saudi Arabian citizen. But a separate attack in the United States, the 1995 bombing of a government building in Oklahoma City, was carried out by an American former soldier, Timothy McVeigh, who believed that the US government was becoming increasingly oppressive, levying heavy taxes, trying to restrict the individual's right to own firearms, and bullying its citizens. A number of US groups, known as militias, shared McVeigh's ideas without resorting to terrorism, but most Americans regarded such ideas as fantasies. McVeigh was executed in 2001.

As these examples suggest, terrorist acts are carried out by people of different nationalities, operating in different ways. Terrorists may be lone individuals or members of large groups. They may operate underground or they may have official backing from a state that allows them to use bases on its territory from which to launch attacks on other countries (this is known as state-sponsored terrorism). And their motives, aims and methods may differ widely from one group or situation to the next.

It is important to study all these different forms of terrorism because something that happens all over the world needs to be explained. When a terrorist act causes the deaths of innocent people, it is tempting just to say that terrorists are evil and leave it at that. But destroying this evil may prove impossible unless we understand how terrorism came to exist.

DEBATE

Do you agree with the Perspectives quotation (page 9) that the use of the term 'terrorist' often involves a value judgement?

2: The Faces of Terrorism

Atrocities have often been committed during wars or periods of persecution, by both governments and their opponents. But until the twentieth century, there was relatively little terrorism in the modern sense, aimed against a society and its leaders. There are many reasons for this, including the limited weaponry available in the past, and the more restricted possibilities of travel. The most common act of terrorism was assassination – the murder of a single, usually important, individual. The first systematic terrorist campaign was probably carried out by a sect that existed between the eleventh and

A contemporary French drawing of anarchist sympathizer Leon Czolgosz shooting President McKinley at the Pan-American Exhibition at Buffalo in 1901. The President died eight days later, and fear of anarchism spread across America.

PERSPECTIVES

'It is not with words or paper that we shall change existing conditions. The last advice I have for true anarchists ... is to arm themselves according to my example with a good revolver, a good dagger and a box of matches.'

Louis Chavès in 1884, before dying in a gun battle against the police

thirteenth centuries in northern Persia. Its followers were regularly sent abroad to kill enemy leaders. They became known as 'Assassins' (Hashshashin), supposedly because they used the drug hashish to prepare themselves for what were bound to be suicide missions.

Many other assassinations have been the work of individuals with personal grievances or religious motives. But killings have also been carried out by people who wanted to destroy tyrants. Over the centuries, thinkers debated whether such a killing was justified, or whether rulers should always be obeyed. It was the first of many difficult issues that would come to be associated with the issue of terrorism.

Modern terrorism

In the late nineteenth century, new ideas and new weapons led to the first terrorist attacks of the modern type, carried out in order to terrify and kill innocent people. The most common weapons were bombs, planted in places such as cafés and theatres. The terrorists were anarchists – men and women who believed that all states and governments were oppressive, and that people could run their own affairs by voluntary co-operation, without any authority over them. Some anarchists concluded that peaceful action could never overthrow the state and the rich and powerful people who controlled it. These anarchists turned to terrorism. Anarchist bombings and assassinations mainly took place in France, Italy and Spain, but in 1901 an anarchist sympathizer shot and killed the US President, William McKinley.

The anarchists were defeated and, for much of the twentieth century, terrorism seemed a relatively unimportant issue by comparison with the great conflicts between states, including the First World War (1914-18) and the Second World War (1939-45).

However, the First World War broke out following a terrorist attack on 28 June 1914, when the Austrian archduke Franz Ferdinand and his wife were murdered at Sarajevo in Bosnia. The assassin, Gavrilo Princip, was a young Serb opposed to Austrian rule in Bosnia, a Serb-inhabited province which he believed should therefore belong to the kingdom of Serbia.

After the Second World War ended in 1945, global politics was dominated by the Cold War. Most of the world was divided into two hostile alliances, representing two contrasting political systems and ways of life. One alliance was led by the USA, and the other by the Soviet Union (a world power much larger than, but dominated by, present-day Russia). As both sides had huge stores of nuclear weapons, fear of a devastating nuclear conflict prevented the outbreak of a world war. But there were a number of smaller-scale wars, and both sides sometimes helped terrorist groups that acted against the other's allies or friends. The Cold War ended in 1991, when the Soviet political system collapsed as a result of its own weaknesses.

Political revolutionaries

From the 1950s, terrorists were sometimes active in African and Asian countries, especially where the peoples of these countries were struggling to win their independence from European powers such as Britain and France. But it was in the late 1960s that terrorism began to spread more widely. By that time, the age of cheap, fast travel had begun and increasingly compact, deadly weapons and bombs could be made or bought. Many small groups were formed that aimed to overthrow the political and economic system in the Americas and Europe. Most of them were radical or left-wing – that is, they favoured some extreme form of socialism, in which the state ran the economy and, it was claimed, there would be equality and social justice. Lacking popular support for such revolutionary change, the groups tried to bring down the existing system through terrorism.

For the first time, car-bombing, hijacking and hostage-taking became international problems. Radical groups sprang up in many countries. Among them were the Red Brigades (Italian), the Red Army (Japanese), the Baader-Meinhof group (West Germany), the Angry Brigade (Britain), and the Tupamaros (Argentina). In the USA, a similar group, the Weathermen, or Weather Underground, grew out of opposition to the US involvement in the Vietnam War in South-East Asia.

These political groups were responsible for many deaths, but few of them managed to operate effectively for long. Most had only a small membership, and their lack of popular support meant that they had few hiding places and were in time trapped by the police and security forces. One of the most notorious gangs of the 1970s was the Red Army Faction led by Andreas Baader and Ulrike Meinhof. Founded in 1968, this West German group supported itself by robbing banks while bombing properties and murdering a number of politicians and businessmen. Their activities made headlines, but by 1972 most of the members were in prison, and in 1976-77 the leaders died in jail, having apparently committed suicide.

One surprising feature of left-wing revolutionary terrorism in the 1970s was that it appeared in so many prosperous, economically advanced nations. In poorer countries, left-wing terrorism proved more persistent, and in the early twenty-first century there were still such groups, usually combining guerrilla activity and terrorism, in countries as different as Colombia and Nepal.

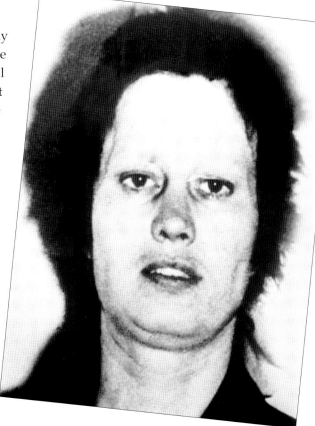

Ulrike Meinhof in 1972, shortly after her arrest for murders committed by her and her gang.

Nationalism and terrorism

Many terrorists claim to represent a nation or people that is being oppressed and should be allowed its independence. Here are some examples. The terrorist organization ETA has waged a long campaign aimed at gaining a separate state for the Basque people of northern Spain. (ETA stands for Euskadi ta Askatasuna, meaning Basque Land and Freedom.) Chechen terrorism (see page 8) followed two wars (1994, 1999) in which Russian armies crushed the Chechens' bid for independence. Chechnya in southern Russia had been conquered by the Russians in the nineteenth century, and only had a chance of achieving independence when the Russian-dominated Soviet Union broke up in 1992. Since 1983, the Tamils of northern Sri Lanka have used both guerrilla and terrorist tactics in their struggle for a separate state from the Sinhalese majority population of the island. Kurdish activities were similarly motivated (see page 9).

Independence issues are often more complicated than they seem at first. Since 1978, Spain has allowed the Basques and other peoples and regions to run almost all of their own affairs. Yet ETA has continued with bombings and assassinations, despite protest rallies and election results showing that the majority of Basques do not support them. Like the political terrorists of the 1970s, ETA members appear to believe that they know better than their own people – not an uncommon belief among terrorists and their supporters.

A 1997 demonstration against ETA violence in Bilbao, the largest city in the Basque region of Spain.

The Troubles

However, the rights and wrongs of such situations are often much less clear. This is certainly the case in the British province

PERSPECTIVES

'The "troubles" emerge not from some random pathological [diseased] desire to ... use violence, but from centuries of extremely complex patterns of politics and oppression.'

Lloyd Pettiford and David Harding, Terrorism: The New World War, *2003*

of Northern Ireland, where violent conflicts of recent times (known as 'The Troubles') are deeply rooted in history. By 1600, England had conquered all of Ireland. This happened at a time of fierce religious hatreds, and Protestant England dealt harshly with the Catholic Irish. Despite later attempts at reconciliation, in 1921 most of Ireland moved towards independence.

However, in parts of the North, Irish Protestants were in the majority. They were the descendants of English and Scottish settlers. They refused to become part of an independent Ireland with a Catholic majority. An artificially created province, Northern Ireland, was set up for them and remained part of Britain.

The Protestants of Northern Ireland became known as Unionists or Loyalists because of their commitment to the British connection. The Catholics, known as Nationalists or Republicans, formed a substantial minority in the province, but for over 40 years they were treated as second-class citizens. The division also had a political and economic aspect, since the Unionists kept complete control over Northern Ireland's parliament, police, jobs and housing.

A civil rights demonstration in Northern Ireland, 1968.

The first effective protests began in 1968, when members of the Catholic minority launched a movement to claim equal civil rights for their community. The hostile Unionist response led to violence on both sides, and British troops were soon sent in. Reforms came too late to prevent terrorist groups on both sides from becoming involved. The IRA (Irish Republican Army) was able to present itself as the protector of the nationalist population, but it also had a wider programme – to 'liberate' the North from British rule and make it part of a united Ireland. Eventually the IRA extended its terrorist campaign to mainland Britain. Its most notorious attacks included the 1984 bombing of the Grand Hotel in Brighton, which narrowly failed to kill the British prime minister, Margaret Thatcher, and her cabinet.

The Troubles went on for decades, and compromise seemed impossible. But signs began to appear that ordinary people in both communities were tiring of the never-ending violence. By 1994 the IRA was ready for a ceasefire, although the peace process continued to suffer setbacks. In April 1998, the Good Friday Agreement was signed by the British and Irish prime ministers and most of the Northern Irish political parties. It arranged for a new form of Northern Irish self-government in which power would be shared between Unionists and Nationalists. They still distrusted each other so much that the British government was forced to suspend the arrangement in 2000 and again in 2003. By 2004 the political difficulties had become very considerable, but in the meantime the province continued to enjoy relative peace.

This painting on the wall of a house in Belfast expresses support for a Unionist terrorist group, the UVF.

Israel and the Palestinians

Some terrorist outbreaks have been explained as the work of desperate people who have no alternative. If they are faced with overwhelming force and have no peaceful, political way of resisting, some of them are almost certain to turn to terrorism. Of course, finding a reason why something happens is not the same as saying that it is justified.

This argument, that 'Terrorism is the weapon of the weak', has often been used in relation to the long-standing conflict between Israel and the Palestinians. Here, too, the issue developed out of a complicated history. By the twentieth century, Palestine, the Jewish homeland in ancient times, had long been mainly inhabited by Arabs. When Palestine was under British rule (1920-48), the number of Jews settling in the country angered many Arabs, and there were serious clashes. When the British left in 1948, the Jews set up the state of Israel in the part of Palestine they controlled. Israel survived invasions by several Arab states in support of the Palestinian Arabs, many of whom were driven or fled from Israeli territory. This created a refugee problem that became a major obstacle to peace between Israelis and Arabs.

Israel soon became a militarily powerful state, defeating its Arab neighbours in three further wars (1956, 1967, 1973). During the 1967 war, Israel occupied the rest of what had been Palestine – the West Bank and the Gaza Strip, both inhabited by Palestinians. The failure of the Arab states left resistance to Israel in the hands of the Palestinians themselves.

Leadership was assumed by the Palestine Liberation Organization (PLO), led by Yasser Arafat. It was committed to the destruction of Israel, and became one of the most notorious terrorist organizations of the 1970s. The PLO, or groups linked to it, carried out many attacks on Israel. But such groups were also responsible for killings in other countries and hijackings involving a number of national airlines. One of the most sensational events of the 1970s was the shooting of eleven Israeli athletes at the 1972 Munich Olympic Games. The group responsible was Black September, at that time part of the PLO.

September 1970: empty American, British and Swiss airliners are blown up in the Jordanian desert. The Palestinian group responsible, the Popular Front for the Liberation of Palestine, exchanged hostages from the airliners for a Palestinian terrorist imprisoned in Britain.

The hijacking of an Air France passenger plane in June 1976 was the work of Palestinians helped by German terrorists. It also ended dramatically, with the hostages rescued by Israeli commandos at Entebbe in Uganda.

The PLO experienced both successes and failures, but the defeat of Israel never seemed likely. By 1988 Arafat was ready to change direction. He announced that the PLO recognized Israel's right to exist and would give up

terrorism. Real progress appeared to have been made in 1993, when Israelis and Palestinians made an agreement at Oslo in Norway. Arafat was to become the head of a Palestinian Authority with limited powers of self-rule in the Occupied Territories, and Israel agreed to withdraw over a five-year period.

However, there were soon new disputes, notably over the Palestinian Authority's failure to stamp out terrorism and the increasing number of Jewish settlements being established on the West Bank. Each side blamed the other, and the same type of deadlock occurred again and again. Israel would not negotiate until Arafat brought terrorism under control, while Arafat blamed the Israeli settlements and Israel's tough security measures for violent Palestinian unrest and renewed terrorist attacks.

Israel claimed that Arafat was not really trying to stop terrorism. If he was trying, he did not succeed. During the 1990s, terrorist attacks were frequently the work of relatively new organizations, such as Hamas and Islamic Jihad, that were not part of the PLO. Their rise marked an important change. Unlike the PLO (a purely political organization), they claimed to base their policies on the religion of Islam, whose followers are known as Muslims. They declared that non-Muslims must not rule any part of the Islamic world, and so they sought to destroy Israel. And, as their followers believed that it was praiseworthy to be a 'martyr' for their faith, some of them were prepared to take part in suicide attacks. A typical incident would involve a man or woman strapping explosives to his or her body and setting them off in a crowded place. After such an incident, Israel generally retaliated by attacking places that were said to be sheltering terrorists, by bulldozing the houses of terrorists' families, or assassinating alleged terrorist leaders outside Israeli territory. This inevitably stoked up Palestinian anger, making the situation even more tense. In 2003 an American-backed effort created a 'road map' for a peaceful end to the conflict, but an outbreak of new suicide bombings made it uncertain whether it could succeed.

Islamist terrorism

Hamas and Islamic Jihad are examples of a trend that grew stronger and far more widespread in the 1990s. The Islamic world is made up of large areas of Africa, the Middle East and Asia – regions where Muslims are in the majority. In many Muslim countries, nationalist, socialist and parliamentary politics seemed to have failed to create much stability and prosperity. As a result, the idea that political action should be based on religious principles became widely popular. New parties and militant groups demanded that the religious law of Islam should become state law, and that non-Muslim influences should be controlled or eliminated. Sometimes labelled 'Islamic fundamentalism', this trend is better described as Islamist.

Masked Palestinian gunmen flourish their weaponry on a march in the West Bank city of Nablus in 2000.

The interpretation of Islam that the Islamists put forward was not necessarily supported by a majority of Muslims. And many Islamists worked non-violently to achieve their aims. Only a minority turned to terrorism, sometimes in response to state terrorism that sparked conflicts between Muslim and Muslim. For example, in Algeria, the radical religious party Islamic Salvation Front made such a successful start in the 1992 elections

PERSPECTIVES

'All Israelis – men, women and children – are forces of occupation. Therefore martyrdom operations are the highest form of jihad [holy war] operations.'

Muhammed Sayyd Tantawi, Professor of International Law at Al Azhar University, Cairo, Egypt

PERSPECTIVES

'The reason so many Muslims are angry is because most of them live under antidemocratic regimes backed by America, with lagging economies and shrinking opportunities for young people.'

Thomas Friedman, Longitudes and Attitudes: Exploring the World before and after September 11, *2003*

that the existing government scrapped the elections and banned the Front. This was followed by years of Islamic terrorism and state terrorism that cost thousands of lives. In Turkey, an Islamist party formed a government in 1996, but in the following year the military intervened to topple it. In Egypt, Islamist terrorists carried out murders of foreign tourists until they were brutally suppressed by government forces.

But Islamist groups were also often hostile to the West. 'The West' and 'western' are useful (though not very accurate!) terms used to describe the world's advanced economies, originally in North America and Europe, but now including parts of the Far East such as Japan. The western way of life was seen as a threat to traditional Islamic values, for example in its emphasis on consumerism and the greater political and social role played by women.

However, there were also more concrete reasons for hostility towards the West. The West, and especially its most powerful nation, the USA, was seen as propping up some of the most undemocratic regimes in the Islamic world, including Saudi Arabia, some Persian Gulf states, and Egypt, because it suited its interests to do so. The Israeli-Palestinian issue probably created the greatest anger, since the USA was a long-time ally of Israel. Rightly or wrongly, even when the USA tried to act as a peacemaker, it was seen as pro-Israeli.

Such resentments led to a number of anti-American terrorist strikes over the years. These became more lethal in the 1990s, and reached the mainland USA. In February 1993, a bomb at the World Trade Center killed six people and injured a thousand others, although it failed to bring down the twin towers. The Islamists charged with the crime came from Egypt, the Sudan and other countries, a sign of the increasingly multi-national nature of terrorist organization.

Al Qaida

By 1996, US investigations increasingly focused on a wealthy Saudi Arabian businessman named Osama bin Laden. In the 1980s, bin Laden's fortune enabled him to train and command volunteers to fight in a US-backed Cold War campaign in Afghanistan, initially against the left-wing Afghan government and later against the Soviet forces brought in to help them. But then bin Laden turned against the USA, initially because US troops were stationed in Saudi Arabia from 1990, originally as a counter to Iraq's invasion of Kuwait. Saudi Arabia was a US ally, but it was also a holy land to Muslims, where (to bin Laden) there should be no armed non-Muslims. In 1991, bin Laden was thrown out of Saudi Arabia, finding refuge first in the Sudan and then, in 1996, in Afghanistan. During this period he was still funding camps where volunteers from many lands were trained in the use of weapons and explosives – but now with the aim of attacking American targets.

The scene following a terrorist attack in Saudi Arabia. Carried out in 2003, it devastated a compound housing foreigners who worked in the country.

Terrorists operate in secrecy, and bin Laden's organization, Al Qaida ('the Base'), remained something of a mystery. It seemed to be a network of linked groups, and it was not always possible to be sure whether Al Qaida or some other Islamist terrorists were responsible for a particular attack. But Al Qaida was generally believed to have carried out two horrific bombings of US embassies in Kenya and Tanzania in August 1998. It probably carried out an attack on the American navy ship USS *Cole* at Aden in Yemen in October 2000, and it was certainly responsible for the most devastating of all terrorist assaults, the destruction of the World Trade Center on 11 September 2001.

Before 9/11, the United States had responded to terrorist attacks with bombings and cruise missiles against countries believed to have sheltered them. But 9/11 completely changed the scale of the American response. US President George W. Bush declared a 'war on terrorism', beginning with an assault on Afghanistan, where an Islamist government, the Taliban, was allowing bin Laden to run Al Qaida training camps. In October 2001, an aerial bombing campaign by the USA and its allies shattered the Taliban and led to its overthrow by Afghan opposition groups in December 2001. Meanwhile, co-ordinated action by many

Osama bin Laden (centre) in Afghanistan in the 1980s.

governments led to a series of arrests that were believed to have greatly weakened Al Qaida.

However, Bin Laden was not captured, and the Bali bombing in October 2002, by a group that probably had links with Al Qaida, showed that Islamist terrorism was still a serious threat. US officials indicated that the 'war on terrorism' might go on for years.

Varieties of terror

In the early twenty-first century, the exploits of Al Qaida and its allies dominated the news. But other forms of terrorism were inspired by religious or moral beliefs. One was a response to the difficult issue of abortion. Opinions differed sharply about when, if ever, it was justifiable to end a woman's pregnancy. In the USA, some people felt that existing laws amounted to allowing the murder of unborn children. Some groups, claiming to be acting on their Christian beliefs, even conducted terrorist attacks on doctors and clinics, causing a number of deaths.

Religious groups with unusual or extreme ideas, often described as sects or cults, have also resorted to terrorism. A belief that the world was about to end apparently motivated some attacks by Japan's Aum Shinrikyo sect which were not directed against any specific enemy. The most serious occurred on 20 March 1995, when sarin gas was released into the Tokyo underground system, killing 12 people and affecting over 5,000 others.

Even issues such as animal welfare and environmental protection have given rise to terrorist acts – in the USA, for example, by the Earth Liberation Front (ELF). So have various anti-government stances and various racial and other prejudices. Clearly terrorism has many faces.

Japanese commuters suffer the effects of sarin gas, released in Tokyo by the Aum Shinrikyo sect in March 1995.

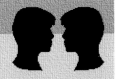

DEBATE

Are there any situations in which terrorism might be justified or unavoidable?

3: Terror Tactics and Weapons

The long-term aims of terrorists may be based on political, nationalist or religious motives, or on some mixture of the three. These will largely determine the kind of tactics and weapons they decide to use.

Generally speaking, terrorists, unlike rebels and revolutionaries, are not hoping for a successful armed uprising against their enemy. Instead, they aim to wear down the authorities and their

CASE STUDY

The most notorious international terrorist of the 1970s and 1980s was 'Carlos the Jackal', whose real name was Illich Ramirez Sanchez. Born in Venezuela in 1949, Carlos was the son of a leftist lawyer. By his early twenties Carlos was involved with radical and pro-Palestinian groups, sharing their aims. Even now, all the facts about his activities are not known, but he is thought to have committed many terrorist acts, including hostage-taking and bombings. He is believed to have been behind the attack on the Israeli athletes at the 1972 Olympics. But he also personally took part in operations. His most sensational coup was to seize 11 oil ministers at a meeting in Vienna, Austria, in 1975. In 1994 Carlos was finally captured in the Sudan and sentenced to life imprisonment for a car bombing in Paris.

'Carlos the Jackal', responsible for terrorist acts all over the world.

In 1946, a Jewish terrorist group bombed the King David Hotel in Jerusalem, which was being used as British Army headquarters.

supporters. If the authorities are hit hard enough and find it impossible to govern, they may become demoralized and give up the struggle or collapse. The terrorists may also try to undermine the economy by attacking tourists or making the country unattractive to foreign firms.

These tactics have sometimes worked, usually when there are other favourable circumstances. For example, in British-ruled Palestine, Jewish terrorism certainly speeded up Britain's decision to leave in 1948. Britain was ruling Palestine on behalf of the United Nations and, weakened by the Second World War, was not sorry to shed a responsibility that brought no benefits with it.

In most instances, however, terrorism has provoked governments to respond forcefully. Among other things, a government will feel it wrong to give in to bullying or blackmail, and it will also lose prestige if it does so. In most cases the result is repeated violence on both sides and a long conflict.

Supporters and rivals

The murder of innocent people causes widespread horror, so terrorists are often isolated. Groups such as the Baader-Meinhof gang and the Red Brigades (see page 14) were condemned by almost everybody, including people with similar political ideals. They were therefore doomed to fail. On the other hand, terrorists may gain a good deal of support among a population that believes it is being oppressed by an outside power. When that power retaliates, the terrorists hope that the people's anger will strengthen support for them. Some popular support is often vital to the terrorists' survival, helping them to find shelter when they are on the run, and making it less likely that people will give them away to the authorities.

From the terrorists' point of view, there is a danger that popular support may dwindle as the violence goes on and on. The oppressed people that the terrorists claim to represent may begin to tire of suffering that seems to bring them no closer to liberation. Then they are likely to turn to a group or party that is willing to operate peacefully, or even to compromise with the 'enemy'. Terrorists tend to claim that there is no alternative to the course they have chosen, but this is often debatable. In many cases the terrorists find themselves rivalled by groups or parties that pursue the same aims by non-violent means.

Nothing is simple in the murky world of terrorism. Sometimes a non-violent, legal party may just be a 'front', an apparently respectable organization that is actually run by terrorist

PERSPECTIVES

'Few of them call themselves terrorists ... They are frequently admired trailblazers. Some of them, in Cuba, Kenya, Cyprus, Israel, have made a transition from hunted insurgent to state president or premier.'

David J. Whittaker, Terrorism: Understanding the Global Threat, *2002*

sympathizers. This front enables terrorists to raise funds and produce propaganda openly. In August 2003 the Basque political party Batsuna was banned on the grounds that it was a front for the terrorist organization ETA. Similar charges have been made about the Northern Irish republican party, Sinn Féin. This is one of the most controversial of terrorist issues. In some cases terrorists may well be operating behind a front organization – but on the other hand it may suit a government to claim that such links exist, using them as an excuse to suppress legitimate opposition.

Terrorists are generally against agreements involving compromise or gradual change, so they may be hostile towards parties that operate legally. They may even use terrorism to disrupt such agreements. In Northern Ireland, when the IRA appeared to be giving up terrorism in return for a political settlement, some of its members broke away and formed a new

Mourners at a service of remembrance in central Omagh, Northern Ireland, held for those who died in the August 1998 bombing, carried out by the Real IRA in an effort to destroy the Good Friday Agreement.

organization, the Real IRA. In August 1998, four months after the Good Friday Agreement, the Real IRA tried to destroy the agreement by planting a bomb in the centre of the Northern Irish town of Omagh. The explosion killed 29 people and badly injured many others. However, instead of ruining the peace process, it caused such horror that the Real IRA was forced to stop its operations for a time. By contrast, efforts to achieve peace between Israelis and Palestinians have often failed because a terrorist attack has provoked a harsh Israeli response. In such situations, unless both sides show great restraint, it is the terrorists who control events.

Instruments of terror

The terrorists' choice of weapons depends on what they hope to achieve in an operation. But they are also influenced by other factors – including the risks they are willing to run.

Any onslaught using hand-guns may score an initial success. But the gunmen have to use their weapons at relatively close range, and risk being shot before they can get away. They can avoid this if they are able to employ mortars and missiles fired from a distance, as was done by the IRA in attacks on police stations, and by Hezbollah and other groups firing from Lebanon or Syria across the border into Israel.

CASE STUDY

In March 2003, US and British armies invaded Iraq. The brutal Iraqi tyrant, Saddam Hussein, was rapidly overthrown. But after their victory, the western occupying forces suffered heavy losses from ambushes and suicide bombings. It was unclear to what extent the attackers were Saddam supporters, Islamists from Iraq or abroad, or ordinary Iraqis opposed to the occupation. Western leaders sometimes called them 'terrorists', and sometimes 'insurgents' (rebels). Their targets even included international humanitarian organizations such as the United Nations and the Red Cross. Consequently most westerners regarded the bombings as terrorist acts; the attackers, however, saw organizations such as the United Nations as partners in a western take-over of the country. However, the attackers increasingly targeted Iraqis who co-operated with the occupiers. And the suicide bombings that killed and maimed innocent bystanders looked more and more like terrorism than armed resistance.

Leon Klinghoffer, 69, poses for a holiday photo taken by a family friend. Klinghoffer was shot and thrown overboard when terrorists seized the Italian cruise ship, the *Achille Lauro*. The partially paralysed New York shop owner was on a wedding anniversary trip with his wife.

Guns are most commonly used by terrorists in hostage-taking. This may involve kidnapping and hiding the victims, seizing a public building, or hijacking an airliner. On one occasion, in 1985, terrorists even hijacked a cruise ship, the *Achille Lauro*. Hijackings win international publicity for the terrorists and their cause; eager to make an impact, they seem indifferent to the anger aroused when the hijackings lead to killings. Sometimes one murder may be enough to outrage the world, as when the terrorists on the *Achille Lauro* shot an elderly, wheelchair-bound American Jew who dared to argue with them.

Terrorist hijackers most often demand the release of their imprisoned comrades, threatening to murder their hostages if the demand is rejected. Kidnapping is similarly motivated. But on some occasions, hostages are held for very long periods before the terrorists decide on their fate. Some are held for years and are eventually released, with or without some concessions by the authorities. But others are quickly murdered. In January 2002 the American journalist Daniel Pearl was working in Karachi, Pakistan, when he was lured into a trap by the promise of a good news story. The terrorists made a brief attempt to bargain for his life, then killed him in a particularly barbaric fashion. In most conflicts, both sides usually allow journalists to operate without becoming targets – but not necessarily, it appears, where terrorists are concerned. Four of Pearl's captors were captured, but the actual killing is believed to have been carried out by a leading figure in Al Qaida, still at large.

PERSPECTIVES

'...terrorists, if they had such material [uranium, used to make nuclear weapons], would have a good chance of setting off a high-yield explosion simply by dropping one half of the material onto the other half... Even a high school kid could make a bomb in short order.'

Veteran atomic physicist Luis Alvarez, writing in Alvarez: Adventures of a Physicist, *1987*

Bombs are the most common terrorist weapons. One of their advantages is that they can be planted and timed to go off later, enabling the terrorists to get away safely before the explosion. To some extent, the bombers can control how lethal their operations are. One US radical group, the Weathermen, planted bombs at night so that military targets would be destroyed without taking human lives. An alternative tactic is to give a telephone warning, leaving the authorities to get everyone out of the target area at short notice, if they can. At the other extreme, terrorists may plant bombs to cause the largest possible number of casualties as well as the greatest possible damage.

Palestinian Hiba Darghmeh, who carried out a suicide bombing in Afula in 2003. She was a student at a West Bank university and a devout Muslim, whose brother, a militant, had been held by the Israelis for nearly a year.

If the terrorist is prepared to die, suicide bombing is a particularly effective way to do this. The terrorist straps explosives to his or her body, where they are hidden beneath a layer of clothing. At a chosen moment, the explosives are detonated in a crowded place, causing terrible carnage. Alternatively, a car loaded with explosives may be driven straight into a target. The increasing number of suicide attacks worldwide since the 1990s is one of the most alarming recent trends. Though suicide bombings have occasionally been used since the 1970s, this tactic has been mainly taken up by Islamists, who regard self-sacrifice as a righteous martyrdom, endured on behalf of their faith.

The destruction of the World Trade Center in 2001 was also a suicide attack, in which the aircraft were used as flying bombs. To seize control of the planes, the terrorists used small but razor-sharp knives, of the type made for jobs like carpet-fitting. But although the world's worst-ever terrorist act was accomplished with low-tech weapons, it is unlikely to be repeated thanks to greatly increased worldwide airline security.

Fears for the future

The number of terrorist acts committed in the world varies from year to year. There is some evidence that the total is tending to become smaller – but that individual acts are claiming more lives, so that the number of victims is actually rising.

The situation could become far worse if, as is widely feared, terrorists ever manage to get hold of weapons of mass destruction (WMDs). These are nuclear, biological and chemical weapons, capable of killing tens of thousands of people and developed, openly or in secret, by many states. Possible sources of supply for terrorists include trade in nuclear materials taken from Russia's poorly maintained facilities; chemicals stolen from US laboratories; and programmes developed by 'rogue states' that do not behave according to normal international standards and sponsor terrorism. So far, such weapons have been used on a relatively small scale – in the Tokyo sarin gas attack (see page 25), and in the sending of five envelopes containing spores of anthrax, a killer disease, through the US mail. The anthrax attack took place only 24 days after 11 September 2001, and killed five people who opened the envelopes and inhaled the spores. The reasons for the attack have never been discovered, but it suggested that fears of biological and other WMDs may not have been exaggerated.

The front page of the *National Enquirer* newspaper, following the October 2001 anthrax attack on their offices in Boca Raton, Florida, which killed one man.

DEBATE

Should a government ever give in to hostage-takers?

4: The Impact of Terrorism

In most of its forms, terrorism brings death and destruction. The natural reaction of ordinary people in a community under attack is of outrage, horror – and fear. Along with fear of violence comes fear of the unknown. Once a terrorist campaign has begun, life-shattering attacks may strike anywhere, at any time. Governments are expected to react rapidly and forcefully.

Security checks

Government efforts to deal with terrorism affect everyday life in many ways. After 9/11, US citizens found themselves subjected to far more thorough security checks at airports. They were even required to remove their footwear, following the 2002 arrest of British Islamist Richard Reid, who boarded an airliner with

Shocked, grief-stricken bystanders in Istanbul, Turkey, after the terrorist bombing of the British consulate on 20 November 2003.

explosives concealed in his shoes. There were other inconveniences. Bags were opened and people had to walk through metal detectors in public buildings. Individuals entering other public places were turned back if they were carrying objects large enough to contain bombs. Cars too became suspect, and garage attendants were liable to insist on a thorough inspection before accepting the vehicle for maintenance or parking.

In the West, people find such conditions annoying. They are accepted because it is hoped they will stop a full-scale terrorist campaign from getting under way. But in many countries a terrorist campaign is already happening, and people suffer more than annoyance. In Israel, suicide bombers have proved highly effective, and many citizens are afraid of performing everyday acts such as boarding a bus. Yet, for most people, daily routines of work, travel and shopping must go on. Commentators often marvel at the way in which everyday life seems unchanged in the most extreme conditions. But this air of normality is an illusion. The changed atmosphere in the United States was shown by the response in August 2003 to an electricity blackout in the north-east – many people

Security, US-style. Armed National Guards watch airline passengers as they pass through metal detectors and X-ray machines at Sacramento International Airport, California, in November 2001.

PERSPECTIVES

Sometimes members of the terrorists' families suffer too.

'At first I blamed myself, then I was angry with them. I remember when I was four-and-a-half, getting off the phone to my mom in prison and thinking through my tears that if only I had been more loveable, if only I could have talked to my parents, I could have stopped them going.'

Statement in the Observer newspaper, UK, by Chesa Boudin, whose parents belonged to the Weathermen group of US terrorists and were given long prison sentences immediately assumed that it was the result of a terrorist attack. Unlike the number of the dead, the stress and anguish generated by terrorism cannot be calculated.

Strengthening the state

Some of the worst ordeals are suffered by people who live under a government with little respect for human rights that is being challenged by guerrillas and terrorists. Then ordinary people are victimized twice over. In Peru, for example, from the 1980s onwards a revolutionary group, the Shining Path, murdered anyone who worked independently for the benefit of the poor – only the Shining Path, supposedly, was entitled to do that. But the same poor people were also regularly raided by the army, which, brutalized by the conflict, arrested, tortured and killed individuals, often without any evidence of wrongdoing.

Abimael Guzman (centre), founder of the Shining Path, is guarded by special forces while being transferred from one prison to another in 1993.

Most western countries have a much stronger tradition of respect for individual rights. But even there, some believe, combating terrorism has given the state dangerously extended powers. Americans were traditionally reluctant to give governments too much power over them, and the provisions of the US Constitution guaranteed citizens protection against abuses of state authority. But in the aftermath of 9/11, many western nations passed laws giving security forces sweeping new powers. In the USA, a 'Patriot Act' was rushed through, despite some protests that it allowed secret searches, arrests and deportations. And in Britain there were complaints that new anti-terrorism laws were being used by the police as an excuse to stop, hold and search people taking part in peaceful, legal demonstrations. Another concern was that government agents would violate individuals' right to privacy by using telephoto lenses and listening devices to spy on anyone they claimed was a suspected terrorist. It remained to be seen just how seriously these concerns would have to be taken.

Similar problems arose over the treatment of suspected terrorists. The western legal tradition insists that nobody should be held for long without being charged and put on trial for a crime. It is even more emphatic that a person is presumed to be innocent until found guilty by a court. When an outrageous terrorist act has just been committed, it is tempting to deal harshly with anyone who is captured or strongly suspected of being involved. But to destroy western principles of justice can be seen as behaving no better than terrorists, who also put themselves above the law. Looked at in this way, it is a victory for terrorism.

However, terrorism does also create new legal difficulties. In October 2001, declaring that they acted in self-defence, the USA and its allies began bombing targets in Afghanistan, a state that had been sheltering Osama bin Laden and allowing him to run Al Qaida training camps. Many prisoners were taken and transported to the US naval base at Guantanamo Bay, Cuba. Their status was uncertain, but the US government denied that they were prisoners of war, who have very specific rights under international law, and described them as 'unlawful combatants'. There were criticisms, inside the USA as well as abroad, of conditions at the prison camp at Guantanamo Bay, the length of time that captives were being held without trial, and the government's intention to hold trials before military tribunals rather than the US courts.

Lockerbie, Scotland, December 1988: the scene of destruction at the crash site of Pan Am Flight 103. The hole dug by the impact of the 747 was about 10 m (30 feet) deep and over 65 m (200 feet) long.

CASE STUDY

At 7.03 p.m. on 21 December 1988, a bomb exploded on Pan Am Flight 103. The stricken airliner plunged down on to the small Scottish town of Lockerbie. All 259 passengers and crew were killed, along with 11 townspeople. Plane debris and human body parts were scattered over a wide area. The people of Lockerbie, even those who lost relations, helped in the search for survivors and the clean-up – although at least one of them afterwards experienced nightmares and flashbacks for years. The experience affected the entire community, and it was ten years before Christmas lights went on again in the town.

Relatives of the passengers and crew visited frequently and established a bond with the townspeople. Destroyed houses were rebuilt, but there was a strong feeling that coming to terms with the tragedy would be impossible until justice was done. 'I want justice – no, let's be honest, I want revenge' cried the father of one passenger. Eventually two Libyans were accused, but the Libyan government gave them up only after years of international pressure. Finally, in January 2001, one of the two was convicted of planting the bomb and sentenced to life imprisonment.

Consequences

Terrorism continues to affect life in all sorts of ways. After 9/11, fewer people were willing to travel by air, and a number of airlines suffered financially. Fewer Americans vacationed in Europe, damaging the tourist industries of countries such as Britain and France. The anti-terrorist war in Afghanistan was one of several conflicts that created huge numbers of refugees who sought asylum in other countries – where they might or

PERSPECTIVES

'Sadly, most Americans do not seem to realize that Congress is about to pass a law that drastically expands government power to invade our privacy, to imprison people without due process [the normal legal procedures], and to punish dissent. More disturbing is that this power grab of our freedoms and civil liberties is in fact not necessary to fight terrorism.'

Letter to the US Congress, sent in October 2001 by the American Civil Liberties Union, an organization set up to protect people's rights against the government or other authorities

might not be welcome. Inevitably, victims of terrorism blamed the communities from which terrorists came. So national, ethnic and religious prejudices tended to spread, even though most governments did their best to counter the trend.

Terrorists may or may not achieve their aims, but their actions affect societies in many ways. And how to defeat terrorism remains a much-debated issue.

Guantanamo Bay, Cuba, January 2002. Captives in orange jumpsuits wait in a holding area of the naval base, known as 'Camp X-Ray', before being taken to their cells.

DEBATE

Do individuals have rights that should not be sacrificed, even in the face of serious terrorist threats?

5: Against Terrorism

Terrorist acts confront governments with some of their most difficult tasks. Many lives depend on the decisions they make at crucial moments. A government may try to defeat the terrorists, to negotiate with them, or to combine these approaches in some way. In every case, misjudgements may bring renewed suffering and death.

Fighting terror

In their efforts to defeat terrorism, states take extra security measures. They issue identity papers and use searches, scans and checkpoints to catch terrorists, if possible before they strike. These methods do not always work, especially against suicide attacks. Complete security may be impossible to achieve – at least, not without giving up a modern way of life based on freedom to travel, trade and settle.

November 2003: an everyday scene at the 350-km security fence built to separate the West Bank from Israel, as a defence against terrorist attacks by Palestinians. Israeli soldiers check the papers of Palestinians who wish to pass through one of the gates.

PERSPECTIVES

'There are days when our fellow citizens do not hear news about the war on terror. There's never a day when I do not learn of another threat or receive reports of operations in progress, or give an order in this global war.'

US President George W. Bush, State of the Union Address, 28 January 2003

Mobilizing skills

Terrorist episodes such as hostage-taking often require an immediate response from governments. Since the emergence of modern terrorism in the 1960s, states have trained negotiators and elite troop units to deal with such situations. The negotiators try to persuade the terrorists not to carry out their threats (for example, to kill hostages or to blow up the building or aircraft they are occupying).

Meanwhile, government ministers have to decide whether or not to make a deal with the terrorists. In many hostage-taking episodes, the terrorists have demanded the release of imprisoned comrades in return for letting the hostages live. This creates a problem for governments. Refusing to make a deal will lead to the loss of innocent lives. But agreeing to the terrorists' demands will give them a victory and, by encouraging them, may cost even more lives in the future. Nevertheless, threats to kill the hostages one by one have sometimes proved difficult to hold out against, especially as fearful relatives of the hostages beg for the non-violent solution. In practice, few governments have been entirely consistent in their responses.

A further option is to use elite troops, often described as special forces. These troops have been trained to act with deadly efficiency, in order to kill the terrorists while minimizing hostage deaths. However, despite the special forces' intensive training, such situations are never entirely predictable.

There have been a few brilliant successes, such as the 1980 SAS rescue of hostages at the Iranian Embassy in London. On other occasions things have gone badly wrong. And the growth of suicide attacks has made these tactics more hazardous. In the 2002 Moscow theatre siege (see page 8), gas was pumped into the building before the special forces went in. The gas did put

CASE STUDY

On 30 April 1980, six gunmen occupied the Iranian Embassy in London and took 26 hostages. They demanded self-government for their province, Arabistan, and the release of political prisoners. While armed marksmen surrounded the building, a team from the British special forces regiment, the SAS, moved into a nearby barracks. On 1 May, at night, an SAS team moved into a building two doors away. The next night, a terrorist statement was broadcast by the BBC in return for the release of some of the hostages – while an SAS team climbed over the roofs and reconnoitred the embassy building. By 5 May, negotiations between the terrorists and the Iranian government were going badly. Shots were heard, and the body of the embassy press officer was thrown on to the pavement, with threats of more to follow. To hold up the executions, police negotiators promised the terrorists a flight out of the country. Then the SAS acted. At 7.23 p.m., eight black-clad servicemen wearing respirators abseiled from the roof to the first floor. They blew in the windows, threw in stun grenades, and followed. The terrorists managed to kill just one of the hostages before being themselves shot down in a brilliantly swift operation.

A member of the SAS poised to enter the Iranian Embassy in 1980.

out of action the women terrorists who had explosives strapped to their bodies, but it also affected the hostages, many of whom died of the effects when their rescue and medical treatment were mishandled.

Inside jobs

When terrorists have been operating in a country for some time, the authorities will make great efforts to track them down. The police and security forces will try to find people with terrorist connections who are willing to sell information. If possible, they will also plant 'moles' (government agents) among the terrorists. The terrorists generally counter these tactics by dividing their organizations into cells – small groups in which only a single member has any contact with other cells. Since they have only a limited knowledge of the movement as a whole, the cell members cannot give away many of its secrets if they are captured or penetrated by a mole. On occasion, however, security forces have been remarkably successful in planting an agent among the very top leaders of a terrorist organization.

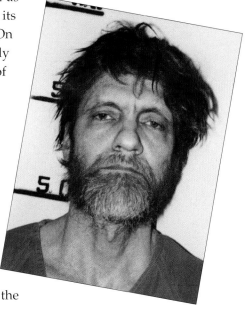

None of these tactics work when a terrorist operates alone. He, or she, is difficult to track down because of this lack of contacts. For 17 years, Theodore Kaczynski, nicknamed the Unabomber, posted letter bombs to US officials as part of a protest against policies that he believed were damaging the environment. He was finally captured only in 1996, through information supplied by his brother.

Pursuit

When an attack has taken place, the authorities pursue the fleeing terrorists. Searches and pursuits now take place across frontiers. After 9/11, there was far greater co-operation between governments to meet the threat posed by terrorism. This made it easier to trace terrorists' movements from country to country, and to seize the banked funds used to finance their activities. Such operations were important, since terrorists often received large sums, from supporters and also from criminal operations such as robberies and drug dealing.

Theodore Kaczynski, known as the 'Unabomber'.

But terrorists who were able to disappear into a friendly population were much harder to trace. Suicide attacks also made the security forces' task even more difficult, since there was little chance of capturing and interrogating the terrorists. One response, adopted by the Israeli armed forces, was to assassinate leaders of organizations such as Hamas, which they regarded as ultimately responsible for attacks. However, like other measures taken against the Palestinians, this policy attracted criticism and its effectiveness was questionable.

Talking with terrorists

Most governments will negotiate with terrorists during an episode such as a hijacking, where lives are at risk. But entering talks about a long-term settlement may be more difficult. Governments have usually denounced terrorists as criminals and murderers – to negotiate with them later on can be seen as giving them recognition or admitting government failure. The families of terrorists' victims are likely to be outraged, and public opinion may be hostile.

Yet in many cases, negotiations have offered the possibility of ending the violence. Where governments have realized this, they have sometimes negotiated in secret while publicly stating that they will never talk with terrorists! The opportunity may well arise after determined action by the government has made the terrorists willing to modify their demands – though they too will probably insist in public that they are standing firm. In Sri Lanka, Northern Ireland and Israel, talks have led to ceasefires and efforts to achieve long-term settlements.

Such arrangements are very fragile, and may be shattered by terrorist acts committed by groups on either side who oppose compromise. Repeated efforts have to be made, usually taking years. And some terrorists may be so absolute in their demands that negotiating with them, and trying to deal with their grievances, would achieve nothing. In the early twenty-first century, that appeared to be true of Al Qaida, though not necessarily of its wider support.

PERSPECTIVES

'The causes [of terrorism] are in the multiple evils of world politics; until these are addressed by those with power to do so, until a lot more good is done, terrorism remains certain.'

Lloyd Pettiford and David Harding, Terrorism: The New World War, *2003*

The challenge

It seems unlikely that any single, simple solution will be found to the worldwide problem of terrorism. Political, national and religious conflicts cannot be magically resolved. It can be argued that 'victory' – the elimination of all terrorism – will never be complete, but that, in the long term, the West could limit the effectiveness of terrorists by creating a fairer world order. If fewer people were poor, hungry and powerless, there would almost certainly be less support for terrorists. Such considerations, though possibly vital, are beyond the scope of this book. What seems certain is that terrorism will continue to be a major challenge to civilization.

US President Bill Clinton (left), Israeli premier Yitzhak Rabin (centre) and Palestinian leader Yasser Arafat (right) at the signing of the Israeli and Palestinian Peace Accord in Washington, DC, USA, in 1993. Secretly negotiated, the Accord made a world sensation when it was announced. But many of the hopes it raised were later dashed.

DEBATE

What is the best way to deal with terrorism? Is there a single 'best' way?

Glossary

Al Qaida a group, or network of groups, led by Osama bin Laden and responsible for 9/11 and other large-scale terrorist strikes.

anarchist a person opposed to all government or state organizations; some, but not all, anarchists have been terrorists.

assassination the murder of a political leader or other prominent person, either for political reasons or because of some real or imaginary grievance.

atrocity a deliberately murderous action, usually involving many deaths.

biological weapons weapons used to spread diseases such as anthrax and smallpox.

chemical weapons weapons using gas, or liquid or solid agents, with the ability to paralyse or kill; employed since the First World War.

civil rights the rights that any citizen can expect to have in a free society.

cult term of disapproval, often used to describe a group with unusual or extreme religious ideas.

guerrillas fighters who generally avoid pitched battles, striking at the enemy with hit-and-run tactics.

Hamas Islamist organization, founded in 1987 and mainly Palestinian-based; responsible for many suicide attacks on Israel.

Hezbollah Middle Eastern terrorist organization, formed in 1982; based in Lebanon, and linked with Iran and Syria, it has carried out many attacks on Israel.

hijacking the violent take-over of an aircraft or other form of transport; the object is usually to take hostages, although on 9/11 the hijacked planes were used as weapons.

Islam the religion of Muslims.

Islamic Jihad Islamist group, mainly associated with carrying out terrorist attacks on Israeli targets.

Islamist Muslim individual or group that believes states must be run on the basis of Islamic religious law (the Sharia).

jihad a holy war – that is, a religious crusade that all Muslims should join. However, it is not at all clear who has the authority to declare a jihad.

left-wing describes people who favour some form of socialism (see below).

legitimate valid and lawful.

martyr a person who dies for his or her religion.

nuclear weapons weapons based on a scientific process by which the nuclei (cores) of tiny particles of matter are split or fused, creating immense explosions of energy; the atomic bomb dropped on Hiroshima in 1945 was the first nuclear weapon to be used.

Palestine Liberation Organization (PLO) organization founded in 1968 to fight against Israel; in 1993 it agreed to give up terrorist activity, and became the main element in the Palestinian Authority intended to create an independent Palestinian state.

radical favouring far-reaching political and/or social changes.

socialism economic system in which industries, and most other forms of wealth, are owned by society, or the state, rather than by individuals or business corporations.

weapons of mass destruction (WMD) weapons, of which a small number are capable of killing huge numbers of people.

Weathermen American revolutionary group, also known as the Weather Underground; founded in 1969, it attacked public (especially military) buildings, until it broke up in the early 1970s.

Useful Addresses

www.bbc.co.uk/learning
BBC Learning – type 'Terrorism' into the search box for an up-to-date list of articles on the subject

www.terrorismanswers.com
Council on Foreign Relations – terrorism: questions and answers

www.cooperativeresearch.org
The Center for Cooperative Research

www.un.org/terrorism
United Nations Action Against Terrorism

Further Reading

Apartheid in South Africa
Sean Connolly
(Heinemann, 2001)

What's at Issue: War and Conflict
Sean Connolly
(Heinemann, 2002)

Lives in Crisis: Conflict in Northern Ireland
Reg Grant
(Hodder Wayland, 2001)

Terrorism
Adam Hibbert
(Franklin Watts, 2002)

11 September 2001
Brendan January
(Heinemann, 2003)

September 2001: Terrorists attack the USA
Patrick Lalley
(Raintree, 2003)

Troubled World: Arab-Israeli Conflict
Ivan Minnis
(Heinemann, 2001)

Why are People Terrorists?
Alex Woolf
(Hodder Wayland, 2004)

World Issues: Terrorism
Stanley Weitzman
(Chrysalis Children's Books, 2004)

Index

Numbers in **bold** refer to pictures.